nice!

Just Cuss a lot

hello

Bye

belongs to: -----

Made in the USA
Monee, IL
15 December 2022

21064397R00066